HOT WHEELS™

S0-ARL-459

THE ULTIMATE HANDBOOK

FUN FACTS, STATS & MORE
ALL ABOUT 150 CARS!

Scholastic Inc.

Hot Wheels®: The Ultimate Handbook is produced by becker&mayer!, Bellevue, WA
www.beckermayer.com

If you have questions or comments about this product, please visit www.beckermayer.com/customerservice.html and click on the Customer Service Request Form.

Written by Sam Negley
Edited by Delia Greve
Editorial assistance by Leah Jenness
Designed by Tyler Freidenrich
Design assistance by Aileen Morrow
Production management by Tom Miller
Product development by Todd Rider
Managing Editorial by Michael del Rosario

Printed, manufactured, and assembled in Shenzhen, China 8/12.

10 9 8 7 6 5 4 3 2 1

ISBN: 978-0-545-49185-3

11913

Special thanks: Tanya Mann, Diane Reichenberger, Christine Chang, Cindy Ledermann, Ann McNeill, Sylvia Garcia, and Matt Emert.

SCHOLASTIC
www.scholastic.com

Published by Scholastic Inc.,
557 Broadway, New York, NY 10012

WELCOME TO THE WORLD OF HOT WHEELS®!

When Hot Wheels® released their first cars in the late 1960s, they not only introduced a new line of toys but also created a product that became a passion for kids and collectors alike. Since those first cars, Hot Wheels® has produced scale models of the most iconic cars from the largest manufacturers in the world. Their teams have designed all-new vehicles from cars that look like creatures with wheels to ones with tricked-out paint jobs.

There are many types of Hot Wheels® vehicles—City Cars, Imagination Cars, Racing Cars, Stunt Cars, and Showroom Cars. These groups include hundreds of vehicles, each with its own unique design. Which one will be your favorite?

Turn the page and race into the world of Hot Wheels®! Dig in to the designs and check out hundreds of stats, fun facts, tips, and tricks for the latest Hot Wheels® cars. While learning about the cars, get a glimpse at Hot Wheels® history, take a look under the hood, and discover what it takes to become a Hot Wheels® collector. Then test your knowledge with some head-scratching trivia and games.

Start your engines and get ready for the ride of your life!

TABLE OF CONTENTS

DID YOU KNOW?

Since 1968, more than 800 models and 11,000 variations (small changes, such as new wheels) of Hot Wheels® cars have been created.

The first 16 cars released by Hot Wheels® in 1968 are known as the Original Sixteen. They include:

- **BEATNIK BANDIT**
- **CUSTOM BARRACUDA**
- **CUSTOM CAMARO**
- **CUSTOM CORVETTE**
- **CUSTOM COUGAR**
- **CUSTOM ELDORADO**
- **CUSTOM FIREBIRD**
- **CUSTOM FLEETSIDE**
- **CUSTOM MUSTANG**
- **CUSTOM T-BIRD**
- **CUSTOM VOLKSWAGEN**
- **DEORA®**
- **FORD J-CAR**
- **HOT HEAP**
- **PYTHON**
- **SILHOUETTE®**

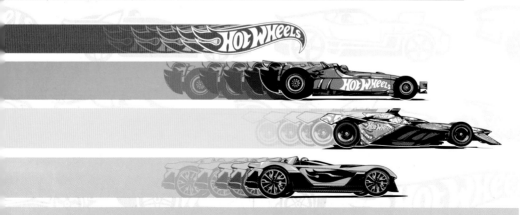

If all the Hot Wheels® vehicles produced in the past 40 years were lined up front-to-rear, they would circle Earth more than four times!

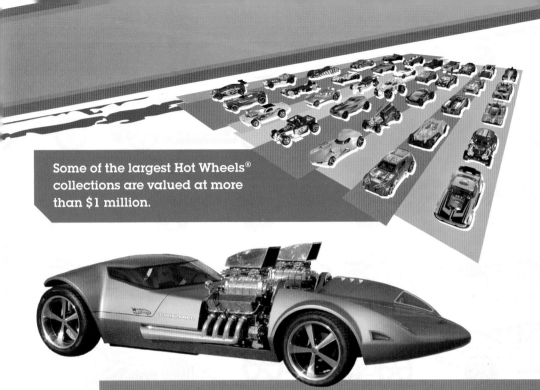

Some of the largest Hot Wheels® collections are valued at more than $1 million.

Hot Wheels® unveiled the first life-sized Hot Wheels® car, called the Twin Mill®, in 2001. It is usually on display in the lobby of the design center at Mattel headquarters in El Segundo, California. The toy version of the Twin Mill® is 1:64 scale.

In 2011, Team Hot Wheels™—a driving team that does stunts in life-sized Hot Wheels® cars—broke the record for farthest jump in a 4-wheeled vehicle by traveling 332 feet (101 m) in the air at the Indy 500 race.

HOT WHEELS® HISTORY

1968 Hot Wheels® releases its first cars.

1975 Motorcycles are introduced into the Hot Wheels® line.

1980s The "blue card" packaging that creates a "wall of blue" in the toy aisle debuts.

1995 The Treasure Hunt Series is introduced.

1997 Hot Wheels® makes models of NASCAR stock cars.

1999 Hot Wheels® begins making models of Formula I cars.

2001 The first life-sized Hot Wheels® car, the Twin Mill®, is unveiled.

2008 Hot Wheels® uses designers from Dodge, Ford, General Motors, Honda, Lotus, and Mitsubishi to create new vehicles in 1:64 scale.

2003 A second life-sized Hot Wheels® car, the Deora® II, is built.

2010 Hot Wheels® Battle Force 5, a 3-D CGI cartoon, is released.

2011 Mattel unveils Team Hot Wheels™—a stunt driving team that performs some of the driving world's most extreme stunts.

UNDER THE HOOD

Fast cars look cool, but have you ever wondered what makes them work? Take a look under the hood of this Impavido 1 and discover the secrets behind one of the world's most electrifying racers!

REAR WING

The carbon-fiber wing pushes the rear wheels onto the track to get maximum grip from the mega-sticky slick tires.

V-10 ENGINE

The awesome lightweight engine pumps out immense power to thrust the car along.

REAR SUSPENSION

The adjustable suspension helps the car blast through corners accurately on every turn.

FRONT BRAKE

The enormous brakes are made from lightweight carbon to slow the car down instantly.

TILTED DRIVER'S SEAT

The driver's seat is angled back to help the driver cope with the amazing acceleration and massive cornering forces.

YOKE-TYPE STEERING WHEEL

The driver controls all the car's trick electronics from buttons on the F1-style steering wheel.

DATA-LOGGING COMPUTER

The car is loaded with electronic sensors linked to a computer to tell the team exactly how it's performing.

RADIATORS

The aluminum radiators cool the hot oil and water pumped through them from the mighty engine.

FRONT SUSPENSION

The super-stiff twin suspension springs help this low-line racer take corners flat-out.

AIR INTAKES

The huge air intakes in the nose swallow outside air to cool the brakes and radiators.

BE A COLLECTOR

Being a Hot Wheels® collector is simple—all you need to do is collect the cars you like. Every Hot Wheels® car belongs to a segment (or group). Each year, there are new segments and hundreds of new car designs. For collectors, it's important to know what kind of cars they have. The easiest way to find out is right on the package.

SEGMENT COLOR

This is an easy way to quickly tell segments apart.

SEGMENT NAME

This is the official name of the segment.

VEHICLE NAME

This is the official name of the vehicle.

TREASURE HUNT CARS

The most exclusive Hot Wheels® cars in the basic car assortment are the Treasure Hunt vehicles. Each year, Hot Wheels® puts out only about 15 different Treasure Hunt cars. These cars have special paint jobs and unique designs, which make them rare. Look for the logo below on Hot Wheels® packaging to find the latest Treasure Hunt cars!

SURF CRATE™

TREA$URE HUNT CARS

Rarer and even harder to find than the Treasure Hunt cars are the Trea$ure Hunt cars. These cars are all metal and have special tires and paint jobs. Hot Wheels® has made these super exclusive cars a true treasure hunt: The packages for these cars do not have a special segment name. You won't know if you have a Trea$ure Hunt car until it is out of the package!

DODGE CORONET SUPER BEE

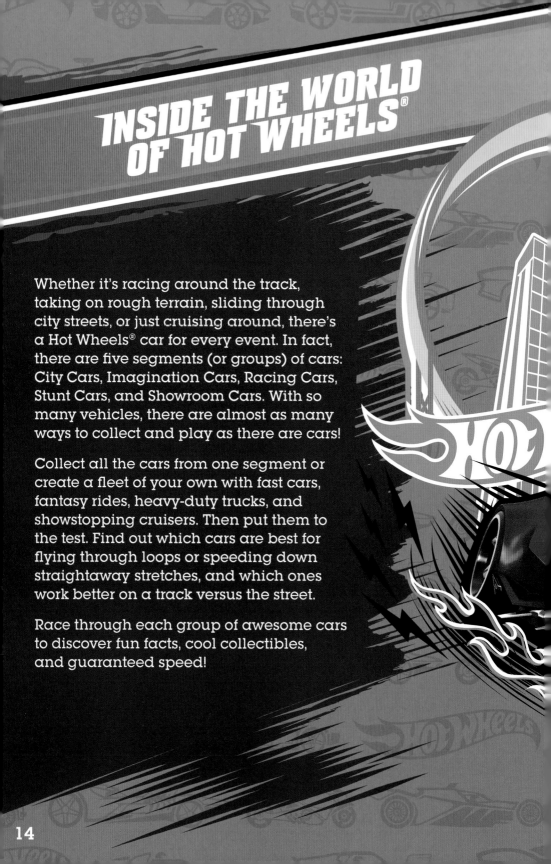

INSIDE THE WORLD OF HOT WHEELS®

Whether it's racing around the track, taking on rough terrain, sliding through city streets, or just cruising around, there's a Hot Wheels® car for every event. In fact, there are five segments (or groups) of cars: City Cars, Imagination Cars, Racing Cars, Stunt Cars, and Showroom Cars. With so many vehicles, there are almost as many ways to collect and play as there are cars!

Collect all the cars from one segment or create a fleet of your own with fast cars, fantasy rides, heavy-duty trucks, and showstopping cruisers. Then put them to the test. Find out which cars are best for flying through loops or speeding down straightaway stretches, and which ones work better on a track versus the street.

Race through each group of awesome cars to discover fun facts, cool collectibles, and guaranteed speed!

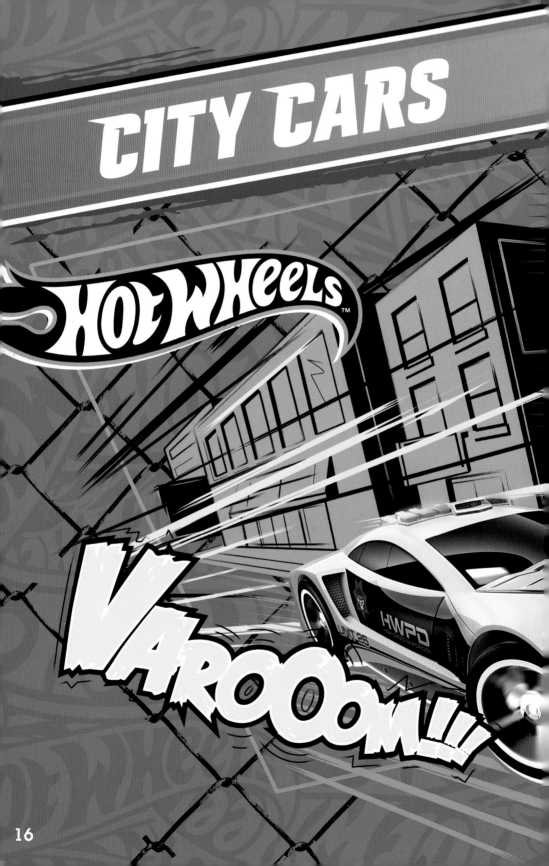

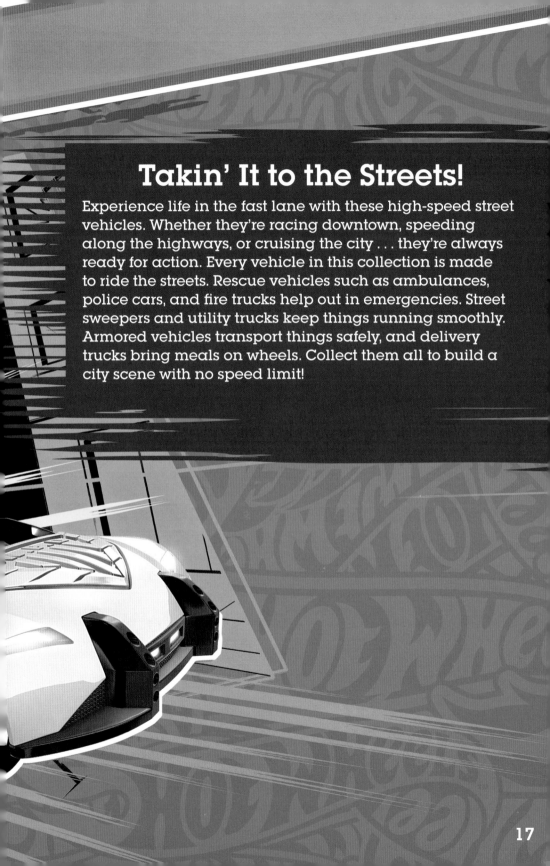

Takin' It to the Streets!

Experience life in the fast lane with these high-speed street vehicles. Whether they're racing downtown, speeding along the highways, or cruising the city . . . they're always ready for action. Every vehicle in this collection is made to ride the streets. Rescue vehicles such as ambulances, police cars, and fire trucks help out in emergencies. Street sweepers and utility trucks keep things running smoothly. Armored vehicles transport things safely, and delivery trucks bring meals on wheels. Collect them all to build a city scene with no speed limit!

CITY CARS

24/SEVEN®

Born: 2002
Birthplace: El Segundo, CA, USA
Designer: Hot Wheels®

Specialty: With a huge rear wing, body kit, and wind splitter, this tuner car races 365 days a year.

5 ALARM

Born: 2009
Birthplace: El Segundo, CA, USA
Designer: Hot Wheels®

Specialty: With a turbine tank engine, side exhaust, and safety tools on top, this fire truck has a fast response on and off the job.

ARMORED TRUCK

Born: 1996
Birthplace: El Segundo, CA, USA
Designer: Hot Wheels®

Specialty: Armor-plated with a V-8 engine, this heavy-duty vehicle was made for fast, secure transport—done with Hot Wheels® style!

FAST FACT
Most armored trucks are equipped to protect whatever they are transporting from being stolen. These vehicles are not only hard to break into, they can flee in a flash!

FAST FACT
An Aston Martin was used in a James Bond movie.

ASTON MARTIN ONE-77

Born: 2008
Birthplace: Gaydon, Warwickshire, England
Designer: Aston Martin

Specialty: It has a full carbon-fiber monocoque chassis, a handcrafted aluminum body, and a naturally aspirated 7.3 liter V-12 engine. Here, the art and vehicle worlds intersect in a stunning—and superfast—limited edition.

19

BACK SLIDER®

Born: 2009
Birthplace: El Segundo, CA, USA
Designer: Hot Wheels®

Specialty: This 6-wheeled transporter has a sliding load ramp that exposes the 8-cylinder engine. It was made for heavy lifting.

BAD BAGGER®

Born: 2006
Birthplace: El Segundo, CA, USA
Designer: Hot Wheels®

Specialty: With dual saddle bags and a V-twin engine, this motorcycle is cruisin' for a bruisin'.

BMW M3 GT2

Born: 2011
Birthplace: Munich, Germany
Designer: BMW

Specialty: Built to race, this high-performance version of the M3 series features a large rear spoiler, wider wheel fenders, and an upgraded 485-horsepower engine.

FAST FACT
BMW stands for Bayerische Motoren Werke.

BREAD BOX™

Born: 2009
Birthplace: El Segundo, CA, USA
Designer: Hot Wheels®

Specialty: Powered by a lightweight, fuel-efficient turbocharged 4-banger, this speedy truck "delivers" every time!

BYE FOCAL® II

Born: 2008
Birthplace: El Segundo, CA, USA
Designer: Hot Wheels®

Specialty: With dual front air intakes, a transparent hood, and two V-8 engines, this car has it where it counts— on top and under the hood.

DELIVERY VAN

Born: 1970s
Birthplace: El Segundo, CA, USA
Designer: Hot Wheels®

Specialty: With a delivery window and large rear bumper, this van delivers first and fast.

DIESEL DUTY®

Born: 2010
Birthplace: El Segundo, CA, USA
Designer: Hot Wheels®

Specialty: Here's a mid-engine, twin-turbo diesel pickup you don't want to encounter in a dark alley. It's confident, convincing, and it gets the job done.

FAST FACT

The Ducati 1098R was available in black, red, and yellow. A special-edition 1098S was made in the colors of the Italian flag— red, white, and green— called *Tricolore*.

DUCATI 1098R

Born: 2008
Birthplace: Bologna, Italy
Designer: Ducati

Specialty: With a single-sided swing arm, distinctive air ducts, and lightweight build, this sports bike performs without parallel.

FAST GASSIN®

Born: 2009
Birthplace: El Segundo, CA, USA
Designer: Hot Wheels®

Specialty: Its 8 vertical stacks, 6 wheels, and 3 axles make this hot-rodded fuel tanker stacked for fast gas haulin'!

FAST FACT
A fire truck, a fire engine, and a fire wagon are actually three different vehicles—each with its own separate function!

FIRE-EATER®

Born: 1977
Birthplace: El Segundo, CA, USA
Designer: Hot Wheels®

Specialty: Complete with water pumps, fire hoses, and ladders, the Fire-Eater® heats up the streets while saving the day.

HONDA S2000

Born: 1999
Birthplace: Tochigi, Japan
Designer: Honda Motor Company

Specialty: Lighter than its predecessor, the Honda S800, with even stiffer structure/suspension tune, stickier tires, special interior trim, and a bolt-on aluminum hardtop, this sleek roadster is ready to cruise.

FAST FACT
In November 1982, the Honda Accord became the first Japanese car manufactured in the United States.

INFINITI G37

Born: 2009
Birthplace: Tokyo, Japan
Designer: Infiniti Motors

Specialty: Modified with custom bodywork, dual exhaust, and all-wheel drive, this car cruises in high-speed luxury.

LAMBORGHINI GALLARDO LP 570-4 SUPERLEGGERA

Born: 2010
Birthplace: Sant'Agata Bolognese, Italy
Designer: Lamborghini

Specialty: With a dynamic look, a lighter body, and tons of power, the Lamborghini Gallardo LP 570-4 Superleggera brings a whole new meaning to the term "super sports car."

FAST FACT
The fastest Lamborghini car in the world—the Murciélago R-GT—has a top speed of over 220 mph (360 km/h).

LOW FLOW®

Born: 2004
Birthplace: El Segundo, CA, USA
Designer: Hot Wheels®

Specialty: With a tapered tail end, cab-over-engine, and 12 windows, this modified bus not only rides low, but also has the speed to match.

MAZDA FURAI

Born: 2008
Birthplace: Irvine, CA, USA
Designer: Mazda

Specialty: With a 450-bhp rotary engine, scissor doors, and futuristic lines, this 2-seat concept car races like the wind.

MEGA-DUTY®

Born: 2001
Birthplace: El Segundo, CA, USA
Designer: Hot Wheels®

Specialty: This 4-door cab is not your average truck. Built for off-roading, hauling, and carrying huge loads, this beast is so far beyond heavy-duty—it's Mega-Duty®. Drive it hard with five of your friends, because this bad boy seats six comfortably.

MONSTER DAIRY DELIVERY®

Born: 2012
Birthplace: El Segundo, CA, USA
Designer: Hot Wheels®

Specialty: The monster truck version of a Hot Wheels® favorite— this bruiser crashes and bashes.

POWER PANEL®

Born: 2002
Birthplace: El Segundo, CA, USA
Designer: Hot Wheels®

Specialty: Skid plates, a front winch, and a V-10 engine make this off-road 4 x 4 rough and rugged.

RAPID RESPONSE

Born: 2009
Birthplace: El Segundo, CA, USA
Designer: Hot Wheels®

Specialty: With crash-rail fenders, a light bar, and Hot Wheels® upgrades, this rescue rod can speed to the scene and save the day.

ROCKSTER®

Born: 2004
Birthplace: El Segundo, CA, USA
Designer: Hot Wheels®

Specialty: Rumble over rock and snow with this off-road SUV—complete with a roof rack, snowboards, and a soft top!

SPEED TRAP®

Born: 2010
Birthplace: El Segundo, CA, USA
Designer: Hot Wheels®

Specialty: With a shield-engine and fully loaded trunk arsenal, this high-speed pursuit vehicle takes control of any situation.

STREET CLEAVER®

Born: 1995
Birthplace: El Segundo, CA, USA
Designer: Hot Wheels®

Specialty: Equipped with a huge rear wing, a blown diesel engine, and a road-grading shovel, this hot-rod city machine cleans up the streets!

SUPER TSUNAMI®

Born: 2001
Birthplace: El Segundo, CA, USA
Designer: Hot Wheels®

Specialty: This race car makes a giant splash on the track with a huge wing for aerodynamics, a smoothed-out body, and a V-8 engine!

SURFIN' SCHOOL BUS

Born: 2001
Birthplace: El Segundo, CA, USA
Designer: Hot Wheels®

Specialty: With 4 rear exhausts, 4 roof-mounted air scoops, and twin V-10 turbo diesel engines, this bus was made for epic surf trips with lots of friends.

FAST FACT

In 2012, Hot Wheels® released a metal model of *The Jetsons* Surfin' School Bus as part of their Hanna-Barbera Nostalgia line.

TOW JAM™

Born: 1997
Birthplace: El Segundo, CA, USA
Designer: Hot Wheels®

Specialty: Its 6 tires, huge towing winch, and side exhausts give this tow truck extra power and lift. It takes on any wreck with style!

IMAGINATION CARS

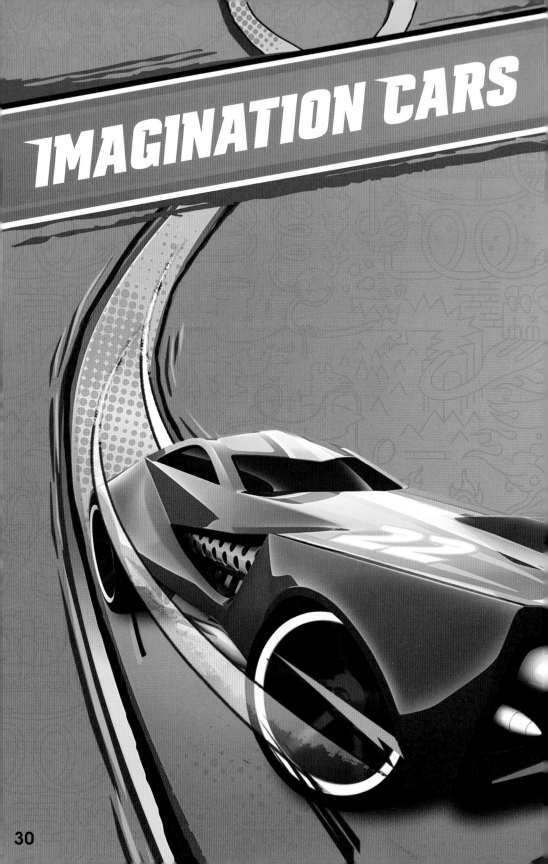

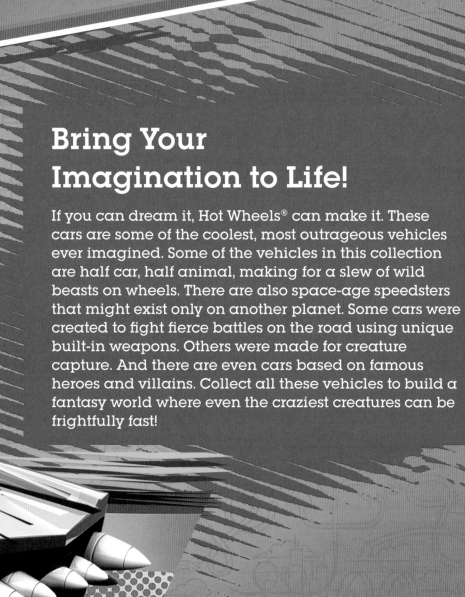

Bring Your Imagination to Life!

If you can dream it, Hot Wheels® can make it. These cars are some of the coolest, most outrageous vehicles ever imagined. Some of the vehicles in this collection are half car, half animal, making for a slew of wild beasts on wheels. There are also space-age speedsters that might exist only on another planet. Some cars were created to fight fierce battles on the road using unique built-in weapons. Others were made for creature capture. And there are even cars based on famous heroes and villains. Collect all these vehicles to build a fantasy world where even the craziest creatures can be frightfully fast!

IMAGINATION CARS

ARACHNOROD®

Born: 2000
Birthplace: El Segundo, CA, USA
Designer: Hot Wheels®

Specialty: This jet-powered racer was built as a tribute to eight-legged creatures everywhere. Its large spider-shaped engine intake gives this hot rod the boost to pounce on any car ensnared in its web.

FAST FACT
Hot Wheels® has created many vehicles that are made to look like spiders and other insects—such as the Speed Spider™ and Scorpedo™.

BAD MUDDER® 2

Born: **2007**
Birthplace: **El Segundo, CA, USA**
Designer: **Hot Wheels®**

Specialty: **This rock crusher takes all-terrain to the next level, with a hood intake scoop, dual stacks, and oversize fenders.**

BUZZERK®

Born: **2010**
Birthplace: **El Segundo, CA, USA**
Designer: **Hot Wheels®**

Specialty: **Powered by its supertorque engine, this is truly a cutting-edge racer. It slices the competition with its circular saw blade and always looks sharp!**

CLOAK AND DAGGER®

Born: **2006**
Birthplace: **El Segundo, CA, USA**
Designer: **Hot Wheels®**

Specialty: **With no windows, covered wheels, and a mini jet engine, this futuristic single-seater is set for interplanetary stealth missions.**

33

CROC ROD™

Born: 2007
Birthplace: El Segundo, CA, USA
Designer: Hot Wheels®

Specialty: Later, gator! This "insti-gator" has a twin supercharged, intercooled engine to give it speed that's off the scales!

FAST FACT

As part of the Color Shifters Creatures line, Hot Wheels® released a version of Croc Rod™ that changed color when dunked in warm and cold water—in or out of the water, this car puts some serious snap in speed.

DRAGGIN' TAIL®

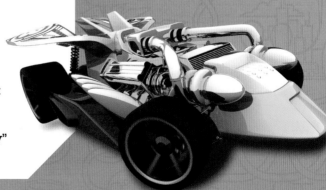

Born: 2009
Birthplace: El Segundo, CA, USA
Designer: Hot Wheels®

Specialty: With an aerodynamic fuselage, a twin turbo V-8 engine, and a pair of wings for downforce, this is one "fly" piece of machinery.

DRIFT KING™

Born: 2007
Birthplace: El Segundo, CA, USA
Designer: Hot Wheels®

Specialty: This 2-seat tuner has an exposed front engine and a huge rear wing for tire screeching and sideways sliding to victory.

EEVIL WEEVIL®

Born: 1986
Birthplace: El Segundo, CA, USA
Designer: Hot Wheels®

Specialty: Its scorpion tail and chomping grille let this creature car take a bite out of its competition.

EL SUPERFASTO®

Born: 2010
Birthplace: El Segundo, CA, USA
Designer: Hot Wheels®

Specialty: Hot Wheels® meets *luchador* in this rolling wrestler! The hardtop "mask" is removable to reveal a translucent body and windshield eyes. It's a sure winner—inside the ring and out!

FAST CASH®

Born: 2010
Birthplace: El Segundo,
CA, USA
Designer: Hot Wheels®

Specialty: The dollar-sign grille, vault doors, combination lock in rear, and metal body make this armored hot rod not just ready to race but also a great money clip or business card holder, too. Check out the chassis for money symbols from around the world!

FORMULA STREET™

Born: 2009
Birthplace: El Segundo,
CA, USA
Designer: Hot Wheels®

Specialty: With a high-performance V-10 engine, a lightweight body, and a front wing for downforce, this car was made for the serious driver with sweet street skills.

H₂GO™

Born: 2008
Birthplace: El Segundo,
CA, USA
Designer: Hot Wheels®

Specialty: With front and rear stabilizer wings and 2 injected V-10 engines, this speedboat is made for hot water pursuits.

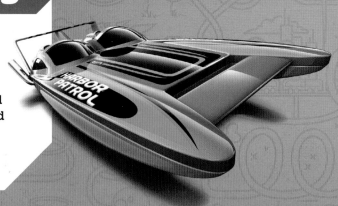

HYPER MITE™

Born: 2001
Birthplace: El Segundo, CA, USA
Designer: Hot Wheels®

Specialty: Fitted with handlebar steering and seating for one, it's small enough to go where no car has gone before. But with 2 V-twin motorcycle engines, it has enough power to make an impression. Try it and you just "mite" like it!

FAST FACT
Hot Wheels® designers get their inspiration for creating original vehicles from a variety of things, including power tools, animals, muscle cars, and so much more.

IMPAVIDO 1™

Born: 2008
Birthplace: El Segundo, CA, USA
Designer: Hot Wheels®

Specialty: Meaning "fearless" in Italian, the Impavido 1™ is a mid-engine exotic supercar with roof scoops and a V-12 engine. It's made for racing and risk taking.

INVADER®

Born: 2005
Birthplace: El Segundo, CA, USA
Designer: Hot Wheels®

Specialty: With a launching rocket and a spinning turret, this tank brings serious speed to combat competition.

JET THREAT® 4

Born: 2006
Birthplace: El Segundo, CA, USA
Designer: Hot Wheels®

Specialty: A flying machine by land and by air, this car has a vertical stabilizer, fold-down wings, and dual jet engines that can transform it from a ground racer to an airborne threat.

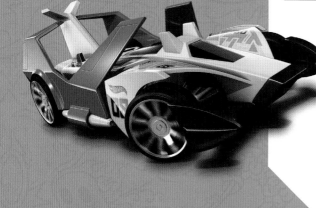

MAD MANGA™

Born: 2012
Birthplace: El Segundo, CA, USA
Designer: Hot Wheels®

Specialty: This anime-inspired speedster features an aggressive long-nose, a chin spoiler, and overfenders. The front-mounted oil cooler and extended exhaust pipes are for both high performance and for makin' a lot of noise!

MAD SPLASH™

Born: 2012
Birthplace: El Segundo, CA, USA
Designer: Hot Wheels®

Specialty: This fast floater owes its heritage to the classic Hot Wheels® favorite Madfast®. It's speedy and agile—on land or water.

RD-05™

Born: 2005
Birthplace: El Segundo, CA, USA
Designer: Hot Wheels®

Specialty: As one of the AcceleRacers® racing drones, this stealthy stalker is built to ride under the radar.

RETRO-ACTIVE®

Born: 2010
Birthplace: El Segundo, CA, USA
Designer: Hot Wheels®

Specialty: With a single cockpit and a built-in single-cell superbattery, this land speed, electric car is charged and ready to roll!

39

ROCKETFIRE®

Born: 2007
Birthplace: El Segundo, CA, USA
Designer: Hot Wheels®

Specialty: This rocket-powered lunar racer wins the space race with aileron guides, airless tires, and gravity-feed fuel pods for extra boost!

FAST FACT

On an airplane, an aileron is a movable surface—usually near the trailing edge of a wing—that controls the roll of the plane to help it bank or turn. On RocketFire®, the ailerons help propel it to victory in the space race!

SCORCHER®

Born: 2006
Birthplace: El Segundo, CA, USA
Designer: Hot Wheels®

Specialty: Cool off the competition with this menace-faced Scorcher®. Its wide-body fender flares and extra-long wing don't just add stability but also make it too hot to touch!

40

SEMI-PSYCHO®

Born: 2005
Birthplace: El Segundo, CA, USA
Designer: Hot Wheels®

Specialty: This semitruck is seriously wild with twin exhaust stacks, a single-seat driver, and 6 wheels to go!

SHARKRUISER®

Born: 1986
Birthplace: El Segundo, CA, USA
Designer: Hot Wheels®

Specialty: With a big fin on top, a sharp grille, and a twin-injected V-8 engine with quadruple exhaust, this is the *carnivore* of the streets!

SKULL CRUSHER®

Born: 2009
Birthplace: El Segundo, CA, USA
Designer: Hot Wheels®

Specialty: Bring on the chills and thrills with this skull-shaped cockpit, rib-cage hood, and grinning grille racer. It's got head-banging speed!

SOLAR REFLEX®

Born: 2006
Birthplace: El Segundo, CA, USA
Designer: Hot Wheels®

Specialty: Let the sun shine down! This solar racer soars past the competition with its dual cockpit, top-mounted solar panel, and a smooth belly pan.

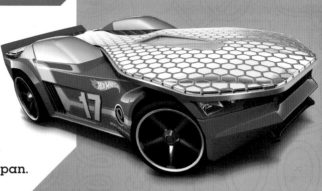

SPECTOR™

Born: 2008
Birthplace: El Segundo, CA, USA
Designer: Hot Wheels®

Specialty: Half robot and half car, this mean machine terminates the competition.

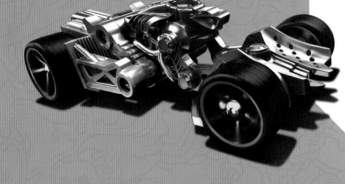

STING ROD™ II

Born: 2010
Birthplace: El Segundo, CA, USA
Designer: Hot Wheels®

Specialty: With a saw blade in the rear, armor plating, and missile launchers mounted on all sides, this beast is always ready for battle!

SWAMP BUGGY

Born: 2009
Birthplace: El Segundo, CA, USA
Designer: Hot Wheels®

Specialty: This bog buggy—with its smooth upper body, oversized shocks, and a giant side opening for fast refueling—is made for a rumble in the jungle.

TREAD AIR®

Born: 2008
Birthplace: El Segundo, CA, USA
Designer: Hot Wheels®

Specialty: Riding on a mono-tread and powered by twin-turbine engines, this single-seat, high-speed off-roader treads where none have tread before.

URBAN AGENT®

Born: 2008
Birthplace: El Segundo, CA, USA
Designer: Hot Wheels®

Specialty: Equipped with projectile missiles and a sight for aiming, this secret-agent car is made for stealthy spying at high speed.

RACING CARS

Drivers, Start Your Engines!

Join the race and zoom past the competition with these unstoppable speedsters. They're quick, sleek, and ready to compete. Every vehicle in this collection is made to test its speed and take on the track. These revved-up racers are equipped with souped-up engines, beefed-up blocks, and sleek styling for extra power and aerodynamic advantage. With cutting-edge technology and high-performance add-ons, these vehicles don't just drive—they fly. Collect them all, and you'll always take the fast track to victory. See you at the finish line!

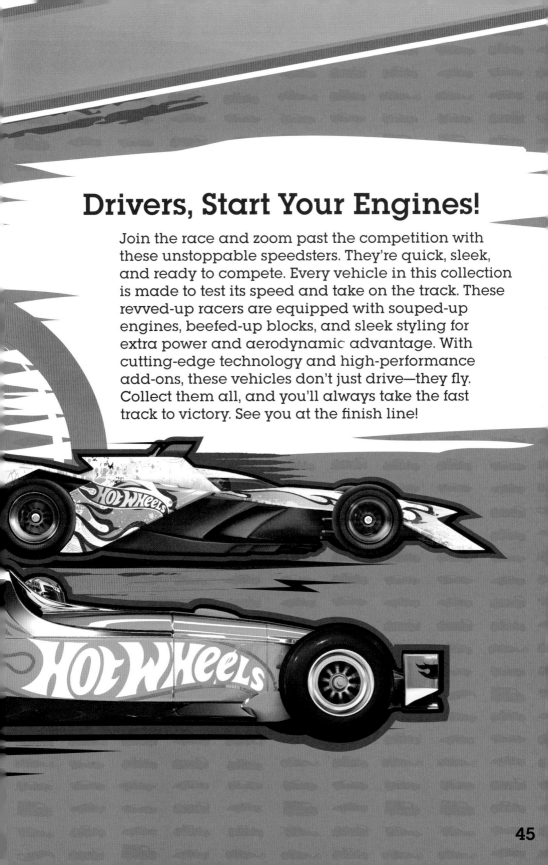

RACING CARS

FAST FACT
An impala is a fast-running antelope that lives in Africa.

'10 CHEVY® IMPALA™

Born: 2009
Birthplace: Detroit, MI, USA
Designer: General Motors

Specialty: Danica Patrick took the IndyCar® world by storm and then set her sights on the Nationwide Series™, driving this high-performance speed machine as #7 in her NASCAR debut at Daytona.

24 OURS™

Born: 2010
Birthplace: El Segundo, CA, USA
Designer: Hot Wheels®

Specialty: With a low-drag body for increased speed, ducting for max airflow, and a V-8 engine, this endurance car takes racing to a new level!

BAD TO THE BLADE™

Born: 2010
Birthplace: El Segundo, CA, USA
Designer: Hot Wheels®

Specialty: Direct from the Hot Wheels Test Facility™ with high-speed wheels and a supertorque engine, this Team Hot Wheels™ racer is truly cutting edge.

BLVD. BRUISER®

Born: 2010
Birthplace: El Segundo, CA, USA
Designer: Hot Wheels®

Specialty: A classic muscle car in body and details—check out that rear spoiler—this power machine is sure to earn major bragging rights on the main drag.

CIRCLE TRACKER

Born: 2009
Birthplace: El Segundo, CA, USA
Designer: Hot Wheels®

Specialty: This stock car of the future combines a cowl-induction hood, a V-8 engine, and a streamlined shape for tearing up the oval track.

CIRCLE TRUCKER®

Born: 2010
Birthplace: El Segundo, CA, USA
Designer: Hot Wheels®

Specialty: Aerodynamically designed to blast around the oval in record time, this truck version of a modern favorite features an oversized cowl-induction hood to give it max power. Its large rear wing keeps it planted on the track for high-speed cornering.

FAST FACT
The Camaro was originally going to be called the Panther.

CUSTOM '11 CAMARO®

Born: 2011
Birthplace: Detroit, MI, USA
Designer: General Motors

Specialty: With a cowl-induction scoop on the hood, a huge rear wing, and a rear diffuser, this road-course racer was made for turning and burning!

48

DIESELBOY®

Born: 2010
Birthplace: El Segundo, CA, USA
Designer: Hot Wheels®

Specialty: With right-hand drive, a clear canopy, side exhausts, and a V-10 engine, this futuristic hot rod was made for high-octane hauling.

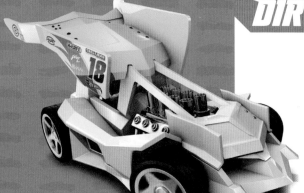

DIRTY OUTLAW™

Born: 2010
Birthplace: El Segundo, CA, USA
Designer: Hot Wheels®

Specialty: This mud slinger sports a big block sidepiece and loves kickin' up a big sideways roost after gunning it down the straights!

F1 RACER

Born: 2009
Birthplace: El Segundo, CA, USA
Designer: Hot Wheels®

Specialty: A high-revving fuel-injected V-8 engine gets this car going. Its front and rear wings and ground effects help it hug the fast track.

F-RACER®

Born: 2003
Birthplace: El Segundo, CA, USA
Designer: Hot Wheels®

Specialty: The huge front and rear wings and the ground effects give this race car maximum stabilization. Strap into the single-seat cockpit, because this racer is made to go *F-AST!*

FAST FELION®

Born: 2008
Birthplace: El Segundo, CA, USA
Designer: Hot Wheels®

Specialty: With European styling and a twin-turbo V-8 engine, this 2-seat GT coupe accelerates through the streets. This is one fast cat!

FAST FISH®

Born: 2007
Birthplace: El Segundo, CA, USA
Designer: Hot Wheels®

Specialty: This Hot Wheels® version of a contemporary muscle car comes equipped with quad exhaust and a transparent hood bulge to show off the brute force of its 8-cylinder engine. It's fast and always fierce.

FIRESTORM®

Born: **2004**
Birthplace: **El Segundo, CA, USA**
Designer: **Hot Wheels®**

Specialty: **Loaded with a jet engine, vertical stabilizers, and a canopy top, this souped-up car is made for a superhero. It's so fast, it "flies."**

FAST FACT

Funny car is a class of drag-racing car. It's so named because on the early models, the rear wheels were moved forward on the chassis, making them look slightly off, or "funny," compared to the original factory versions.

FUNNY SIDE UP™

Born: **2012**
Birthplace: **El Segundo, CA, USA**
Designer: **Hot Wheels®**

Specialty: **This smiling speedster has a flip-up body with classic styling and a top-fuel engine designed to hit 300 mph (483 km/h) in 4.5 seconds. It's a standout dragster—and that's no joke!**

51

GROWLER™

Born: 2012
Birthplace: El Segundo, CA, USA
Designer: Hot Wheels®

Specialty: *Grrrrr . . .* Choke-collar styling, along with a vicious front grille and a bone-shakin' V-8 engine, make this canine-inspired muscle car one bad dog.

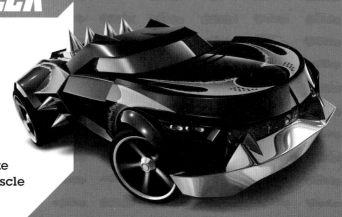

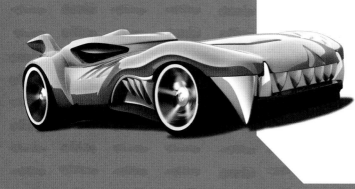

HOWLIN' HEAT®

Born: 2009
Birthplace: El Segundo, CA, USA
Designer: Hot Wheels®

Specialty: With big fangs, big eyes, and dual exhaust, this nocturnal cruiser was made to creep and sweep the competition.

MADFAST®

Born: 2008
Birthplace: El Segundo, CA, USA
Designer: Hot Wheels®

Specialty: Lose your mind in this dragster! Its enclosed cockpit and a blown engine, make it go *insanely* fast!

NERVE HAMMER®

Born: **2006**
Birthplace: **El Segundo, CA, USA**
Designer: **Hot Wheels®**

Specialty: **Disappear into the night! With an exoskeleton structure, transparent bodywork, and a classified engine, this upscale model is fit for a spy.**

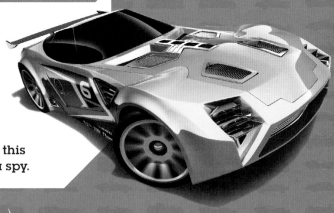

FAST FACT
Nitromethane, also known as nitro, is made specifically as fuel for drag racing so cars can move *fast*. It's the result of a chemical reaction between nitric acid and propane.

NITRO DOORSLAMMER®

Born: **2007**
Birthplace: **El Segundo, CA, USA**
Designer: **Hot Wheels®**

Specialty: **This nitrous-injected dragster is the future of drag cars—pumped with speed and attitude. The flip-out wheelie bar keeps it grounded while it soars past the competition.**

53

OFF-TRACK®

Born: 2004
Birthplace: El Segundo, CA, USA
Designer: Hot Wheels®

Specialty: The all-terrain pickup with a custom chrome-moly frame and an aluminum big-block custom engine is up for anything!

PROTOTYPE H-24®

Born: 2007
Birthplace: El Segundo, CA, USA
Designer: Hot Wheels®

Specialty: Go the distance in this endurance vehicle. With lightweight construction and a 16-cylinder engine, this car doesn't ever want to stop.

FAST FACT:
One of the most famous long-distance auto races is held every year in Le Mans, France. A team of drivers races for 24 hours!

RENNEN RIG™

Born: **2010**
Birthplace: **El Segundo, CA, USA**
Designer: **Hot Wheels®**

Specialty: *Rennen* is German for "racing." Designed for the European truck-racing circuit, this rig is loud—and there's no stopping it!

SPLIT DECISION®

Born: **2005**
Birthplace: **El Segundo, CA, USA**
Designer: **Hot Wheels®**

Specialty: **With body length, flip-up doors, and lightweight, high-strength construction, this futuristic car was made for showing off—and** *showing up* **the competition.**

SPLIT VISION®

Born: **2006**
Birthplace: **El Segundo, CA, USA**
Designer: **Hot Wheels®**

Specialty: **Take a spin on the fast track with this open mid-engine roadster. Its integrated roll bar, side intakes, and V-12 engine push speed to the next level!**

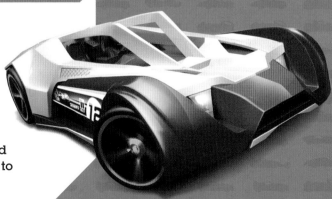

SUPER BLITZEN®

Born: 2010
Birthplace: El Segundo, CA, USA
Designer: Hot Wheels®

Specialty: *Blitzen* is German for "flash," and that's just what this superfast, superstylin' sedan is designed to be. With a rooftop air scoop for superior intake and a low center of gravity, this racer is both fast *and* spectacular.

SUPER COMP DRAGSTER

Born: 1998
Birthplace: El Segundo, CA, USA
Designer: Hot Wheels®

Specialty: The ultimate drag racer! This sleek little car sweeps across the finish line, leaving the competition in the dust!

TORQUE TWISTER™

Born: 2009
Birthplace: El Segundo, CA, USA
Designer: Hot Wheels®

Specialty: With a fuel-injected V-8 engine, a rear diffuser, and dual exhausts, this contemporary muscle car knows how to flex its muscles.

WHAT-4-2®

Born: 2004
Birthplace: El Segundo, CA, USA
Designer: Hot Wheels®

Specialty: Created as the sequel to the Hot Wheels® original What-4, this single-seater has 4 blown engines instead of 2—because if 2 is good, then 4 is better!

FAST FACT:
The original What-4 came out in 1971.

YUR SO FAST®

Born: 2010
Birthplace: El Segundo, CA, USA
Designer: Hot Wheels®

Specialty: Finally, a Hot Wheels® original car that starts with the letter Y! With a 12 biturbo powerplant, a roofless cockpit, and a huge center exhaust to vent all that power, there's no need to ask why it's so fast!

STUNT CARS

Ready for a Thrill Ride?

This collection of cars features extreme vehicles made to re-create the most outrageous stunts, jumps, and over-the-top action! There are motorcycles for maneuvering through canyons and soaring off mega jumps, drift cars for sliding into stunts and cutting across corners, and muscle cars for pure adrenaline-fueled freestyle racing. All the cars in this collection are built with the power to take on the most insane challenges—and with the adrenaline to break world records. Collect them all and be the ultimate daredevil!

STUNT CARS

AMAZOOM™

Born: 2008
Birthplace: El Segundo, CA, USA
Designer: Hot Wheels®

Specialty: Cruise the concrete jungle in this Brazil-inspired race car. With a ground effects package, race suspension, and a roll bar, it's made to ride the river of speed.

BARBARIC®

Born: 2009
Birthplace: El Segundo, CA, USA
Designer: Hot Wheels®

Specialty: This demolition muscle car has integrated armor on the front and a steel rail across the top for smashing through toll gates and busting up the streets.

BLAST LANE™

Born: 2000

Birthplace: El Segundo, CA, USA

Designer: Hot Wheels®

Specialty: With supersleek, custom bodywork and a road-burning V-twin engine, this motorcycle puts life in the fast lane!

FAST FACT

When taking a tight turn, 75% of a sport bike's grip comes from the front tire.

CANYON CARVER®

Born: 2007

Birthplace: El Segundo, CA, USA

Designer: Hot Wheels®

Specialty: Built for precise maneuvering, this speedy sport bike can race down winding country roads, zigzag through rush hour traffic, or cut corners and creep through back alleys with the greatest of ease.

61

CITROËN C4 RALLY

Born: 2009
Birthplace: Paris, France
Designer: PSA Peugeot Citroën

Specialty: Its turbocharged engine produces 420 lbs of torque, making this unreal rally racer born to win.

FAST FACT

In 1967, Citroën introduced swiveling headlights—lighting that changes based on speed and direction—in many models, which resulted in greater visibility on winding roads.

COOL-ONE®

Born: 2004
Birthplace: El Segundo, CA, USA
Designer: Hot Wheels®

Specialty: Originally designed as a souped-up ice-cream truck, this hot-rod van sports chrome exhausts, oversized rear wheels, and serious style.

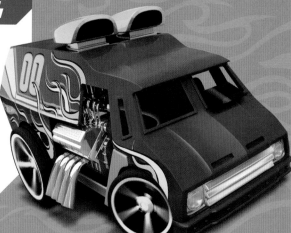

DA'KAR™

Born: 2002
Birthplace: El Segundo, CA, USA
Designer: Hot Wheels®

Specialty:
With a raised body for tough terrain, massive fenders, and a single-seat cockpit, this road warrior is made for battle on any turf.

DODGE CHALLENGER DRIFT CAR

Born: 2011
Birthplace: Auburn Hills, MI, USA
Designer: Chrysler Group LLC

Specialty: This speedy sports car—with a huge rear wing, special body work, and its race car interior—is made for burnin' out sideways!

FORD FIESTA

Born: 2012
Birthplace: Dearborn, MI, USA
Designer: Ford Motor Company, with help from Ken Block

Specialty: This re-creation of a Ken Block gymkhana drifter is ready for some awesome stunt action!

FRIGHT BIKE®

Born: 2001
Birthplace: El Segundo, CA, USA
Designer: Hot Wheels®

Specialty: With a ground scraper and its transparent body, this modified motorbike unleashes terror in drag-racing duels.

GO KART

Born: 1998
Birthplace: El Segundo, CA, USA
Designer: Hot Wheels®

Specialty: Put your driving skills to the test! This single-seater with big rear tires and a 2-stroke engine is made for sheer amusement!

FAST FACT

The first go-kart was built in 1956 by Art Ingels out of scrap parts and an old engine.

GREASED GREMLIN

Born: 1979
Birthplace: Auburn Hills, MI, USA
Designer: Chrysler Group LLC

Specialty: This supermodified, old-school special is designed to tear up the strip in style.

FAST FACT

Hot Wheels® designed a 6-wheeled model of the AMC Gremlin called Open Fire with the extra pair of wheels under a giant, exposed metal engine.

HW40®

Born: 2007
Birthplace: El Segundo, CA, USA
Designer: Hot Wheels®

Specialty: Flex your driving muscles in this Hot Wheels® original! With a jet-turbine engine, a seamless body, and a one-piece glass hood, it's made for aggressive driving.

JEEP SCRAMBLER

Born: 1980
Birthplace: Auburn Hills, MI, USA
Designer: Chrysler Group LLC

Specialty: With off-road tires, 4-wheel drive, and a toolbox and an ax in the bed, this trailblazer is built to tame the jungle.

FAST FACT
Former president Ronald Reagan drove a Jeep® Scrambler on his ranch.

MAD PROPZ®

Born: 2004
Birthplace: El Segundo, CA, USA
Designer: Hot Wheels®

Specialty: This low-wing stunt plane is a flight club favorite. Made for barrel rolls and superloops, Mad Propz® is all about mad fun.

NIGHT BURNER®

Born: **2006**
Birthplace: **El Segundo, CA, USA**
Designer: **Hot Wheels®**

Specialty: **This vehicle's massive turbine engine spins as you blow into it. Give it a whirl to hear the high-pitched scream. It's sure to scare the competition!**

POWER SANDER®

Born: **2003**
Birthplace: **El Segundo, CA, USA**
Designer: **Hot Wheels®**

Specialty: **With its roll cage, lift kit, and rear engine, this single-seater is made for spinning up sand and dredging up the dunes.**

QUICKSAND™

Born: **2012**
Birthplace: **El Segundo, CA, USA**
Designer: **Hot Wheels®**

Specialty: **Pavement or dunes, dirt or track—this desert racer is up for anything. Its long travel suspension, twin-turbo V-8 engine, and armor-platelike body make it willing and able.**

67

ROLL CAGE™

Born: 2000
Birthplace: El Segundo, CA, USA
Designer: Hot Wheels®

Specialty: This buggy was made to roll. Go desert racing and dune bashing with reckless abandon in this rear-engine 2-seater. Shake the sand from your pants and race across the beach in this speedy open-air carriage. Roll play has never been so much fun!

SCOOPA DI FUEGO®

Born: 2009
Birthplace: El Segundo, CA, USA
Designer: Hot Wheels®

Specialty: With huge rear scoops, a wraparound windshield, and sleek design, this Italian-inspired futuristic car is on fire!

SKY KNIFE®

Born: **2006**
Birthplace: **El Segundo, CA, USA**
Designer: **Hot Wheels**®

Specialty: **Fly by day or by night in this helicopter with a bubble canopy, enclosed turbo fan, and turbine engine.**

SNOW RIDE®

Born: **2009**
Birthplace: **El Segundo, CA, USA**
Designer: **Hot Wheels**®

Specialty: **This is no sleigh ride! With extra-wide rack, an 1100 cc 2-stroke engine, and mono shock, this snow ride does *not* take it easy.**

SPIDER RIDER™

Born: **2009**
Birthplace: **El Segundo, CA, USA**
Designer: **Hot Wheels**®

Specialty: **You won't catch this "terrantula" as it flies past! With dual turbocharged 4-cylinder engines, 4-wheel drive, and a roll cage, this vehicle has all the power of eight legs!**

SUBARU WRX STI

Born: 2011
Birthplace: Ota, Gunma, Japan
Designer: Fuji Heavy Industries Ltd.

Specialty: Reaching speeds of up to 158 mph (255 km/h), this turbocharged all-wheel-drive sports car doesn't just own the road—it *challenges* it, too.

SYNKRO®

Born: 2004
Birthplace: El Segundo, CA, USA
Designer: Hot Wheels®

Specialty: This member of the Teku® team of AcceleRacers®—with its huge rear wing, partially exposed engine, and body kit—tunes out the competition!

TRI & STOP ME®

Born: 2008
Birthplace: El Segundo, CA, USA
Designer: Hot Wheels®

Specialty: With a sleek frame, a single rear tire, and Hot Wheels® suspension, this 3-wheeler was made to *tri*umph over the competition.

TWINDUCTION®

Born: 2010
Birthplace: El Segundo, CA, USA
Designer: Hot Wheels®

Specialty: Built to race, this high-performance model features a large rear spoiler, wider wheel fenders, and an upgraded 485-horsepower engine.

TWIN MILL® III

Born: 2008
Birthplace: El Segundo, CA, USA
Designer: Hot Wheels®

Specialty: First released in 1969, this is the third version of the crowd favorite. It's sleek, superfast, and built to win—the ultimate twin-engine racer!

XS-IVE®

Born: 2000
Birthplace: El Segundo, CA, USA
Designer: Hot Wheels®

Specialty: With 6 tires, roll bars, and a roof-mounted kayak, this turbine-powered truck comes to the rescue in all types of weather!

SHOWROOM CARS

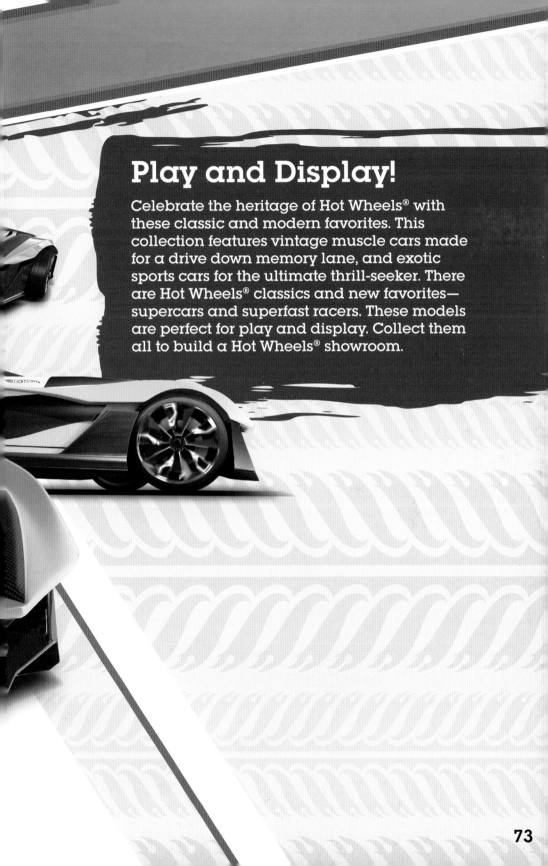

Play and Display!

Celebrate the heritage of Hot Wheels® with these classic and modern favorites. This collection features vintage muscle cars made for a drive down memory lane, and exotic sports cars for the ultimate thrill-seeker. There are Hot Wheels® classics and new favorites—supercars and superfast racers. These models are perfect for play and display. Collect them all to build a Hot Wheels® showroom.

SHOWROOM CARS

'66 CHEVY® NOVA™

Born: 1966
Birthplace: Detroit, MI, USA
Designer: General Motors

Specialty: With chiseled good looks including a bold grille and its semi-fastback roofline, this car is one mean muscle machine that's made for street fighting.

'69 CAMARO®

Born: 1969
Birthplace: Detroit, MI, USA
Designer: General Motors

Specialty: This classic convertible, with covered headlights and a cowl-induction hood, is just the ticket for racing to the beach.

'69 CHEVELLE™ SS™ 396

Born: 1969
Birthplace: Detroit, MI, USA
Designer: General Motors

Specialty: Long, wide, and packed with a V-8 for punch, this classic muscle car makes a statement anywhere it goes.

FAST FACT
The Chevelle SS represented Chevrolet's entry into the muscle car battle.

'69 CORVETTE®

Born: 1969
Birthplace: Detroit, MI, USA
Designer: General Motors

Specialty: With classic Corvette® styling, a lighter body, and a beefy all-aluminum engine block, the elusive ZL-1 has raced its way into history and *mystery* books.

'69 DODGE CORONET SUPER BEE

Born: 1969
Birthplace: Auburn Hills, MI, USA
Designer: Dodge

Specialty: Watch for the bee logo on the back when this muscle car buzzes by—its powerful engine (optional HEMI®!) and heavy-duty suspension give it an edge.

'69 MERCURY COUGAR ELIMIMATOR

Born: 1968
Birthplace: Dearborn, MI, USA
Designer: Ford Motor Company

Specialty: This fast cat eliminates the competition with a hood scoop, a rear spoiler, and a 4-barrel V-8 engine.

'70 BUICK® GSX™

Born: 1970
Birthplace: Detroit, MI, USA
Designer: General Motors

Specialty: With a hood-mounted tachometer and front and rear spoilers, this muscle car is made to take the streets—and to take your pinks.

'70 MONTE CARLO™

Born: 1970
Birthplace: Detroit, MI, USA
Designer: General Motors

Specialty: With an extra-long hood, concealed windshield wipers, and a 4-barrel V-8 engine, this sporty street racer was made for speed.

'70 PONTIAC® GTO®

Born: 1970
Birthplace: Detroit, MI, USA
Designer: General Motors

Specialty: This aggressive GTO® was made to lay down the law on speed!

FAST FACT
It's often said that the age of the muscle car began with the Pontiac GTO®, originally released in 1964.

'71 DODGE DEMON

Born: 1971
Birthplace: Auburn Hills, MI, USA
Designer: Chrysler Group LLC

Specialty: With dual hood scoops, dual exhaust, and a 4-barrel carburetor, this speed demon is made for the mean streets.

'71 PLYMOUTH ROAD RUNNER

Born: 1971
Birthplace: Auburn Hills, MI, USA
Designer: Chrysler Group LLC

Specialty: This baby handles and corners like a dream. With its increased wheelbase and a rear sway bar in place of the staggered leaf springs, it can run any road.

'72 FORD GRAN TORINO SPORT

Born: 1972
Birthplace: Dearborn, MI, USA
Designer: Ford Motor Company

Specialty: Take a "grand" stand in this muscle car. With a V-8 engine, dual exhaust, and a hood scoop, it's made for speed!

'73 PONTIAC® FIREBIRD®

Born: 1973
Birthplace: Detroit, MI, USA
Designer: General Motors

Specialty: Set the road on fire! With a super-duty 455 V-8 engine and its signature egg-crate grille, this high-performance bird knows how to fly!

'83 CHEVY® SILVERADO™

Born: 1983
Birthplace: Detroit, MI, USA
Designer: General Motors

Specialty: Sculpted for a stylish ride, this smooth, customized "heavy half" hauls to the races or to the road.

'86 MONTE CARLO® SS™

Born: 1986
Birthplace: Detroit, MI, USA
Designer: General Motors

Specialty: With a cowl-induction hood, dual exhaust, wide rear tires, and a V-8 engine, this street-legal drag-racing machine puts the *car* in Carlo.

'92 FORD MUSTANG

Born: 1992
Birthplace: Dearborn, MI, USA
Designer: Ford Motor Company

Specialty: Run wild in this classic update. With a small-block V-8 engine, dual exhaust, and a raised cowl-induction scoop, this modified Mustang dishes out sweet street defeat.

FAST FACT
Within the first day of its release on April 17, 1964, Ford sold 22,000 Mustangs.

'10 FORD SHELBY GT-500™ SUPER SNAKE®

Born: 2010
Birthplace: Las Vegas, NV, USA
Designer: Shelby American, Inc.

Specialty: With a special hood, a supercharged V-8 engine, and a gladiator stance, this Super Snake *ssssspeeds* straight past the competition.

8 CRATE®

Born: **2003**
Birthplace: **El Segundo, CA, USA**
Designer: **Hot Wheels®**

Specialty: **With a V-8 engine and rear fin fenders, this wagon is made for classic cruising.**

ASTON MARTIN DBS

Born: **2007**
Birthplace: **Gaydon, Warwickshire, England**
Designer: **Aston Martin**

Specialty: **This British speedster—with its carbon-fiber deck lid, front fenders, and a V-12 engine—knows how to race in style.**

BONE SHAKER®

Born: **2006**
Birthplace: **El Segundo, CA, USA**
Designer: **Hot Wheels®**

Specialty: **A classic hot rod comes to life— or to the afterlife—in this stripped-down Larry Wood–designed truck rod. The skull grille and skeleton hands around the headlights make it a menacing opponent.**

CHEVY® SILVERADO™

Born: 2007
Birthplace: Detroit, MI, USA
Designer: General Motors

Specialty: This customized truck is business in the front, and a party in the back. The slammed Silverado™ hauls a sport bike in the bed for impromptu road races of the 2- or 4-wheeled kind.

FAST FACT
The Chevy® logo is also known as the "bowtie."

CORVETTE® STINGRAY® CONCEPT

Born: 2008
Birthplace: Detroit, MI, USA
Designer: General Motors

Specialty: Based on the original 1959 Stingray® race car, this concept car combines Corvette® cues from other generations with a futuristic shape, making a sweet transformation from old to new.

CUSTOM '64 GALAXIE 500

Born: 1964
Birthplace: Dearborn, MI, USA
Designer: Ford Motor Company

Specialty: With its custom trim, bucket seats, a floor-mounted transmission shifter, and a standard V-8 engine, this custom Hot Wheels® model is in a galaxy of its own.

FANGULA®

Born: 2009
Birthplace: El Segundo, CA, USA
Designer: Hot Wheels®

Specialty: Take a bite out of racing in this killer ride! This auto body features an exposed engine, tall injector stacks, side pipes, and a transparent roof.

FISH'D & CHIP'D™

Born: 2003
Birthplace: El Segundo, CA, USA
Designer: Hot Wheels®

Specialty: With a chopped and lowered roofline, this original luxury car is made for sleek and stylish stints on Broadway.

FORD GTX1

Born: 2005
Birthplace: Dearborn, MI, USA
Designer: Ford Motor Company

Specialty: With a powerful engine and smooth lines, this open-top race car was made for quiet, high speed cruising.

HONDA CIVIC SI

Born: 2006
Birthplace: Tochigi, Japan
Designer: Honda Motor Company

Specialty: This sport-injected Civic is the ultimate tuner Honda. Screaming with attitude, this turbocharged ride proudly flaunts a body kit and a massive rear wing.

JADED®

Born: 2005
Birthplace: El Segundo, CA, USA
Designer: Hot Wheels®

Specialty: Equipped with a parachute, wheelie bars, and a large wing, this powerful hot rod stays in control even at extreme speeds. If you're in another car, take a good look—because all you'll see is the giant rear spoiler flying past.

LAMBORGHINI AVENTADOR LP 700-4

Born: 2011
Birthplace: Sant'Agata Bolognese, Italy
Designer: Lamborghini

Specialty: Named for a trophy-winning bull, this spirited champ uses F1-style suspension on a lightweight carbon-fiber monocoque. It's fast, rare—and it screams luxury.

PORSCHE 911 GT3 RS

Born: 2003
Birthplace: Zuffenhausen, Germany
Designer: Porsche AG

Specialty: A genuine race car that is also street legal, this is truly a high-performance sports car. It's superlight, superfast, and ready for anything. Bring it on!

TAIL DRAGGER®

Born: 1997
Birthplace: El Segundo, CA, USA
Designer: Hot Wheels®

Specialty: With side pipes, fender skirts, and a V-8 engine, this custom, '40s car is made for draggin' its tail up and down Main Street.

WANNA RACE?

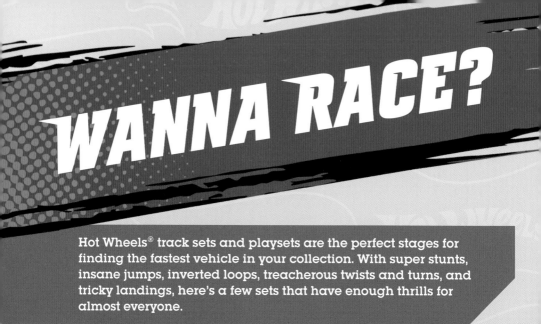

Hot Wheels® track sets and playsets are the perfect stages for finding the fastest vehicle in your collection. With super stunts, insane jumps, inverted loops, treacherous twists and turns, and tricky landings, here's a few sets that have enough thrills for almost everyone.

SHARK SLAMMER™

Power-launch vehicles into the corkscrew curve with the Shark Slammer™ set. Jump through the shark's mouth for a scary-cool finish. This shark likes his meals on wheels!

T-REX TAKEDOWN™

Take a trip back in time with this Jurassic playset. Race through the chomp zone or get caught in the trap door. Escape the piranha pit and rescue trapped cars. Slide down the tail ramp and take down the dino!

MEGA LOOP MAYHEM™

Crashing just became fun! This ultimate set has 2 huge loops, 3 thrilling crash zones, over 13 feet of track, and 2 levers to control when the speeding cars get released from the loops. Test cars solo—or see how many cars you can get racing through the loops at once for a huge crash!

DOUBLE DARE SNARE™

Put your cars to the test against Team Hot Wheels™! The mission: Beat the blue driver and be saved by the supersnare! The set has dual-vehicle launch assist units, vehicle rescue snare, exit jump, and an inverted free-fall jump. It takes precision and timing to beat the competitor through this matrix loop—or else plummet off the cliff.

WALL TRACKS™

Hot Wheels® Wall Tracks™ sets bring speed, stunts, turns, and tricks to new heights. Wall Tracks™ are wall-mounted track play systems for a whole new way to put cars to the ultimate test. Connect different sets together to expand Wall Tracks™—and to launch stunts and action all over the walls.

Speed to victory!

Watch out for the trap door!

RACING DUEL™

For the first time ever, you can race two cars side-by-side down the wall! The set is easy to hang. Load two cars at the starting gate at the top and see which is faster. The slower car falls through the trap door and down to the ground, while the winner races to victory. You can connect the set to other Wall Tracks™ sets, or even to a track set on the floor!

Race them down the wall.

Load cars at the start gate.

POWER TOWER™

The spiral corkscrew elevator of the Power Tower™ set swiftly lifts Hot Wheels® vehicles up to the track's starting point. Once the car is released on to the track, it has multiple obstacles to get around, including a moving saw and a car-chomping monster. Cars that conquer the track are brought back up the elevator for another round—and cars that are "eaten" by the monster fall through the trap door.

HOT WHEELS

BALLISTiKS ™

Create the ultimate rumble with these transforming daredevil ball cars. Ballistiks™ vehicles transform from a ball to a car upon impact. A combination of firepower and attitude, these cars are ready for anything. Issue a challenge; then take down the competition with firepower, skill, and fast-paced battling action. With endless ways to play, the only question is: How do you roll?

FERENZO®

BALLISTIKS™ COMBAT CANNON

Bring out the big gun! It's a vehicle-transforming super-assault weapon. Load your Ballistiks™ vehicle into the launcher. Pull back on the lever and watch the vehicle transform into a ball as it gets ready to fire. Pull back the lever even farther and blast your Ballistiks™ through the launch tube. Upon impact, the ball transforms back into a vehicle and races away.

BALLISTIKS™ CHARACTERS

Collect all 24 characters including . . .

CHUM CHASER™

TOP SPEED GT®

TIRE FRYER™

TRY THESE GAMES

HEAD-TO-HEAD

1. Use chalk or a small piece of paper to mark a center spot on the ground.
2. Aim and shoot your Ballistiks™ vehicle toward the center at the same time as your opponent.
3. After the dust settles, the Ballistiks™ vehicle closest to the mark is the winner!

TURBO TARGETS

1. Use chalk or small pieces of paper to mark targets around the play surface.
2. Aim and shoot your Ballistiks™ vehicle toward the targets. The Ballistiks™ vehicle closest to each target earns a point.
3. After 10 shots, the player with the most points is the winner!

TRIVIA QUIZ

(Answers are on the bottom of page 93.)

1 Which car is this detail from?

2 When were the first Hot Wheels® cars released?

BONUS: What are the first cars released known as?

3 How many models have been created since 1968?

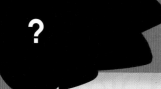

?

4 Which car is designed to look like a spider?

5 How many of the featured City Cars in this book are motorcycles?

BONUS: How many of *all* the featured vehicles in this book are motorcycles?

6 Which car is this detail from?

7 Which car is this detail from?

8 How long was the world-record jump set by Team Hot Wheels™?

9 Which toy company makes Hot Wheels® cars?

10 If positioned front-to-rear, how many times would all the Hot Wheels® vehicles produced in the past 44 years circle the earth?

11 Which car is made to race in sand?

1. Fast Gassin'®; **2.** 1968; **BONUS.** The Original Sixteen; **3.** More than 800 models; **4.** Arachnorod®; **5.** There are 2 motorcycles in City Cars; **BONUS.** There are 5 motorcycles featured in this book; **6.** Hyper Mile™; **7.** '69 Mercury Cougar Eliminator; **8.** 332 feet; **9.** Mattel; **10.** More than 4 times; **11.** Roll Cage™

MEET TEAM HOT WHEELS™

Team Hot Wheels™ is made of four teams—Team Red, Team Blue, Team Green, and Team Yellow. These drivers, who are some of the most fearless in the world, create and perform never-before-seen speed- and gravity-defying stunts. Each team has a unique driving style. Get to know each one!

TEAM RED

Driving style: Wild and daring, Team Red takes on the craziest stunts, such as jumping planes and riding walls.

OUTRAGEOUS ATTITUDE

TEAM YELLOW

Driving style: Team Yellow's motto is "go big or go home." This team is up for any challenge—as long as it pushes the limits!

RAW POWER

TEAM GREEN

Driving style: FAST! Swift, speedy, and in control, Team Green goes for top velocity when performing its stunts.

UNSTOPPABLE SPEED

TEAM BLUE

Driving style: Team Blue is super precise. With skill and timing, it performs every stunt perfectly.

PERFECT PRECISION

automotive wings: Air passes over these to generate downforce—or downward thrust—making the car more stable as it gains speed.

block (as in *beefed-up block*): The engine block, which holds the cylinders and their components inside a cooled and lubricated crankcase. It is designed to be extremely strong and sturdy, because failure of the engine block results in failure of the car.

blown engine: An engine that is equipped with a supercharger, also known as a *blower*.

chassis: The base frame of a car or other wheeled vehicle.

coupe: A car with a fixed roof, two doors, and a sloping rear.

cowl-induction hood: An opening in the hood that forces air into the engine to help it run better.

deck lid: The cover over the trunk that allows access to the main storage or luggage compartment.

dragster (drag car): An automobile designed and built specifically for drag racing.

drifter: A car designed to slide when the driver uses throttle, brakes, clutch, gear shifting, and steering to keep the car in a high-turn angle.

fender skirts: Pieces of bodywork on the fender that cover the upper portions of the rear tires.

grille: A grating at the front of a car allowing air to circulate to the radiator to cool it.

hardtop: A car designed to look like a convertible but still having a rigidly fixed, hardtop.

hot rod: Slang term for a car specially built or altered for fast acceleration and increased speed.

low-drag body: The design of a car that produces less drag so it can go faster.

monocoque chassis: A vehicle construction in which the body and chassis form a single unit.

muscle car: A flashy sports car with a large, powerful engine.

overfenders: Also known as *fender flares*, they are common on pickup trucks to block mud and stones, and to cover rust.

scoop (as in *roof scoop, air scoop*): An aerodynamic device or opening used to duct cool, outside air to some part of the car, such as the engine air intake, the brakes, or the radiator.

side exhaust: An exhaust pipe designed to carry toxic gases away from the car, specifically out the side rather than the back.

spoiler: An air deflector usually mounted at the rear of a car to reduce lift at high speeds.

tachometer: An instrument measuring revolutions per minute on a car engine.

torque: A force that produces rotation.